THE
TWENTY-THIRD

Psalm

~for~
Those Wh

CARMEN

To Christina and David.
I know you still miss
Merrill and always will.

presented to:

from:

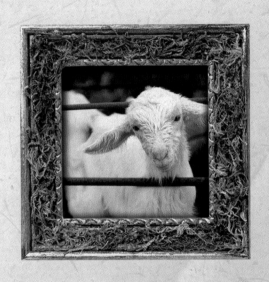

THE
Twenty-Third
Psalm

for
Those Who Grieve

Contents

"Expect to have hope rekindled. Expect your prayers to be answered in wondrous ways."
—Sarah Ban Breathnach

Introduction

THROUGH THE DARK

As a child, Betty could not remember a time when she had not been afraid of the dark. She spent many nights lying in her bed, her heart pounding so loudly that she couldn't tell if someone or something was waiting to pounce. After she memorized Psalm 23 at vacation Bible school one summer though, her situation rapidly improved. At bedtime, instead of imagining all sorts of bad things happening, she'd recite the psalm. As soon as she said, "The Lord is my shepherd, I shall not want," her heart would resume its normal rhythm, her eyes would close, and soon she'd fall asleep, safe in the arms of the Shepherd.

In her late teens, she finally met the Shepherd of her nights and discovered that He was more than just a remedy for fear. He became her Lord and her Savior. The darkness no longer held any terrors for her.

For men are not cast off by the LORD forever. Though he brings grief, he will show compassion, so great is his unfailing love.
—Lamentations 3:31, 32

Many years passed. Then one day Betty, a married mother of four children, faced news that pitched her into a different kind of darkness. Her oldest daughter, Lisa, had died in a car wreck. Instantly, Betty's phobia of the dark returned, this time as a fear of the torment she experienced trying to fall asleep. *What if while I sleep my mind manages to forget that Lisa is gone?* The thought of reliving the searing pain of receiving that awful news each time she woke turned Betty into an insomniac.

Betty panicked when she could not find the peace that reciting Psalm 23 had brought so many years earlier. Every night those comforting words seemed lost in the maelstrom of thoughts Lisa's death had created. Psalm 34:17 reads, "The righteous cry out, and the LORD hears them." As she lay awash in tears, she cried out and the Shepherd heard her cry. This one line broke through her grief: "Even though I walk through the valley of the shadow of death." Only this one line, yet it was enough.

Betty was in the valley of the shadow of death, an even scarier blackness than that she experienced in her childhood bedroom. One word above all gave her hope. *Through*. She didn't have to live in the valley, nor would she die there. The Shepherd had promised that he would walk with her through the valley. He was with her. If she clung to Him, He would bring her out the other side—into the light, into life, into remembered love and joy.

To lose someone we love, as Betty did, alters our lives forever. Some people say it takes a year to get over the resulting grief, but there is no set timetable. A mother doesn't easily get over the death of a child she carried in her womb. It's natural to grieve when a beloved spouse or baby dies, or when a dear friend passes away. Grief is a process. When someone we love dies, his or her uniqueness leaves a hole in our hearts that is his or her exact shape. We can never fill that hole. We can never get over it. But with the Shepherd's help, we can get through it.

The LORD is my shepherd,
I shall not be in want.
He makes me lie down in green pastures,
he leads me beside quiet waters,
he restores my soul.
He guides me in paths of righteousness for his name's sake.
Even though I walk through the valley of the shadow of death,
I will fear no evil, for you are with me;
your rod and your staff, they comfort me.
You prepare a table before me in the presence of my enemies.
You anoint my head with oil; my cup overflows.
Surely goodness and love will follow me all the days of my life,
and I will dwell in the house of the LORD forever.

PSALM 23

CHAPTER ONE

THE SHEPHERD WHO *Cares*

"THE LORD IS MY SHEPHERD"

GOD IN A PAPER BAG

"Bye, Mom. See you later!" The door slammed and twelve-year-old Chucky hopped on his bicycle to deliver newspapers for his best friend, who was out of town.

Minutes later, the newspapers lay scattered over an intersection two blocks away. A car crashed into the side of Chucky's bicycle, tossing him high into the air. Slamming back onto cement pavement, he lay motionless, and, perhaps mercifully, unconscious.

For his father, Chuck, that night seemed to last forever. There were not enough back issues of dog-eared, tear-stained magazines in any hospital's

The LORD is close to the brokenhearted and saves those who are crushed in spirit.
—Psalm 34:18

waiting room to ease his anxiety during the almost seven-hour neurosurgery.

"Everything has been done that we know to do," said the primary neurosurgeon. "Your boy has suffered severe brain damage. He may die soon, or he may not."

Chucky did not die soon. He suffered seizures and further neurosurgery, living in hospitals and rehabilitation centers. Then his grieving parents nursed him at home for nine months. Day after day, facing an

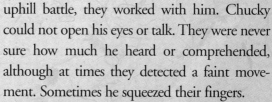

uphill battle, they worked with him. Chucky could not open his eyes or talk. They were never sure how much he heard or comprehended, although at times they detected a faint movement. Sometimes he squeezed their fingers.

As time passed Chuck grieved, prayed, and wondered why the Shepherd appeared to be sleeping on the job. Of course God was not sleeping, but it took a special series of wake-up calls, in the form of plain, brown paper bags, before Chuck finally believed that.

After the accident, every fourth or fifth day, he or his wife began finding a paper bag of fresh fruit on their front doorstep. No note. No card. No name. Sometimes there were a few bananas, an orange or two, and several apples. Other times there were pears, peaches, and grapefruit.

As a result of those anonymous brown paper bags, Chuck began paying attention to what was happening around him. In their own manner, and in a variety of verbal as well as nonverbal ways, family, friends, and even strangers were rallying to encourage the family. It took awhile, but it dawned on Chuck that the Shepherd was not silent or sleeping. God was revealing Himself, offering His love and strength, through all those people.

Chuck also realized that God, using people and things, was helping Chucky, too. His son was loved and receiving good medical and nursing care. Doctors assured them that although Chucky still had the capacity to feel physical pain, he was not in pain. But he didn't wake up. Chucky remained comatose for two years and three months. Then, quite suddenly, on New Year's Day morning, he died. But he was not alone.

Eventually Chuck and his wife learned the identity of the fruit bearer. He was someone they hardly knew, the kind of man who isn't noticed in a room full of people. He was a man of few words and was sort of a loner.

When Chuck thanked that man for all the wonderful fresh fruit, and the sentiment behind those gifts, Chuck doesn't remember him saying anything. He just looked at Chuck, smiled, and firmly shook Chuck's hand.

Aesop, a writer of simple fables, said, "No act of kindness, no matter how small, is ever wasted." Even when Chuck's grief made the thought of food unappealing, when he couldn't eat a piece of fruit, it wasn't wasted.

The great thing to remember is that, though our feelings come and go, His love for us does not.

—C. S. Lewis

The Shepherd used the quiet man's kindness, wrapped in paper bags, to bring comfort to a grieving family.

People see God every day,
they just don't recognize him.
—Pearl Bailey

When he has brought out all his own, he goes on
ahead of them, and his sheep follow him because they
know his voice.
—John 10:4

SAVIOR, LIKE A SHEPHERD LEAD US

DOROTHY A. THRUPP

Savior, like a shepherd lead us, much we need Thy tender care;

In Thy pleasant pastures feed us, for our use Thy folds prepare.

Blessed Jesus, blessed Jesus! Thou hast bought us, Thine we are.

Blessed Jesus, blessed Jesus! Thou hast bought us, Thine we are.

CHAPTER TWO

THE
SHEPHERD WHO

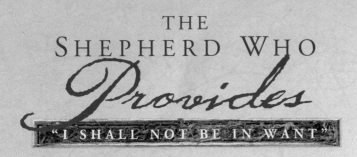

Provides

"I SHALL NOT BE IN WANT"

THE BRACELET PROMISE

Amidst the crowd of holiday shoppers, I made my way to the corner of the store reserved for fine jewelry. In a solitary display case I gazed on a bracelet I knew was a one-of-a-kind treasure; dozens of dark green emeralds, combined with beaten silver that resembled diamond chips.

As I stared in wonder at this intricate piece, I remembered a promise my husband, David, had made four years earlier during our honeymoon. He had selected an emerald-green, Austrian-crystal-and-seed-pearl bracelet in honor of my May birthstone. As he fastened it on my wrist, he lovingly said, "I promise you that soon I will buy you real emeralds. Just wait."

Before they call I will answer; while they are still speaking I will hear.
—Isaiah 65:24

Although I loved the honeymoon gift, deep down I looked forward to the fulfillment of David's promise.

Whenever David saw my bracelet, he remembered his promise and reassured me that he would keep it.

Through the years we continued to look in jewelry store windows as if we were searching for the Holy Grail. We wandered into countless shops, and I became discouraged when I realized that the cost of fulfilling David's promise was well beyond our means. I wavered in my belief that I would own what David desired to give me. David, however, never lost faith.

Now we were in the mall during the last week before Christmas to buy gifts for other people. Finances were tight; we had agreed not to exchange gifts between ourselves. We had just completed a most stressful year during which David had been diagnosed with a terminal, neurological disorder followed by his being dismissed from work due to poor performance. Because of no insurance, we had to pay for all of David's medication and expensive tests. Our financial situation grew desperate.

Worse than the financial stress was the ongoing grief of losing my best friend in bits and pieces. The forgetfulness, irrational anger that exploded unbidden, indecipherable handwriting, and personality changes took their toll on both of us. In fact, sometimes I even envied wives who had lost their husbands in automobile accidents or through fast-moving cancers. I erected barriers around my heart to steel myself against the inevitable loss. Then, just when I persuaded myself that the neurological changes in David had become permanent, he'd have a good day and come close to being his old self. I'd fall in love with him all over again, only to watch him slip away. The grief that washed over me often brought me to my knees to cry out my anguish to the Shepherd.

That day in the mall I looked up from the display case into David's eyes and saw love shining even brighter than the emeralds. I could tell that in his mind nothing less than this bracelet would satisfy his honeymoon promise. I also knew there was no way we could afford it. I tried to tell him no, but the words died on my lips. He'd had so many disappointments this year.

As the store clerk lifted the bracelet out of the case and reached around my wrist to close its intricate clasp, I prayed it would be too small. That would be the easiest way of refusing the bracelet since the unpaid bills, and the promise of more to come, had placed a vise around our checkbook. But God had other plans that day. The bracelet fit perfectly.

I glanced at David and saw his radiant smile burst forth. This man, I thought, is the victim of one of the cruelest diseases known to man. He faces a sentence with only one verdict—an untimely death. My eyes brimmed over with tears as I realized anew we would not live out our dream of growing old together.

To David, this is not just a piece of jewelry. This is his love displayed on my arm for the entire world to see. To him, a promise made is a promise kept. He might not have many more months or years to keep his promise. Somehow I have to juggle the bills to let him have the honor of keeping it.

The clerk reached for my arm to remove the bracelet. I could not believe it had worked its way into my heart so quickly. "How much is it?" I finally asked. Slowly, he turned over the little white tag which read $250.00.

The clerk began to extol the bracelet's virtues pointing out the 180 emerald chips in a hand-made Brazilian setting. It might as well have been $2,500.00 given our meager budget. Knowing that

Faith is putting all of your eggs in God's basket, then counting your blessings before they hatch.
—Ramona C. Carroll

shops in malls do not normally bargain I still asked, "Would you take $225.00, tax included?" With a questioning look he answered, "That will be fine."

Before he could change his mind I whipped out my credit card, watching as David beamed with pride. Soon we were on our way. Every few steps, we stopped to look at the bracelet. Before we reached the

car, David said, "When I get sicker and eventually die, you need to look at each emerald. Each one will remind you of something special we've done—a trip we took, a movie we saw, a moment we shared. This will be your memory bracelet."

I began to cry. David's concern was not for his failing health but for how I would handle life without him.

As we drove our way home in bumper-to-bumper traffic, I wondered how we could pay for the bracelet. We talked as we traveled, every so often looking at the miracle of the promise kept.

On the way into the house I grabbed the mail. Amidst the usual bills were two Christmas cards. The first, from a church where I had sung several times that year, contained a thank-you note for my music ministry along with an amazing gift— a check for $200.00! I then opened the second card, and out fell two bills: a twenty and a five. The card was simply signed, "A friend in Christ."

Even as we shopped in the mall, the payment for David's promise had been in the mailbox. The Shepherd had already taken care of every detail. The pastor of a small church, coupled with an unknown friend, had listened to the Shepherd as they decided their holiday giving. Only because of the Shepherd had we stopped at that shop on that day to find that specific bracelet. The promise David had spoken on our honeymoon had been fulfilled.

Waiting for someone to die is a unique grief that

people can't fully understand unless they have experienced it. Some days I felt as if no one else could ever cry because I had used all their tears too. When my grief blinded me to my blessings, I'd look at my bracelet and remember David's faith and the Shepherd's love.

My bracelet is a piece of jewelry I obviously could have lived without. Yet, when I look at each chip I pull out precious memories that are tucked away in my heart. I also hold onto the Shepherd's promise that he will never leave me and will provide for my every need. After all, he provided a promised piece of jewelry.

Memories, important yesterdays, were once todays.
Treasure and notice today.
—Gloria Gaither

Delight yourself in the LORD and he will
give you the desires of your heart.
—Psalm 37:4

HIS EYE IS ON THE SPARROW

CIVILLA D. MARTIN

Why should I feel discouraged, why should the shadows come,

Why should my heart be lonely, and long for heaven and home,

When Jesus is my portion? My constant friend is He;

His eye is on the sparrow, and I know He watches me;

His eye is on the sparrow, and I know He watches me.

I sing because I'm happy, I sing because I'm free,

For His eye is on the sparrow, And I know He watches me.

CHAPTER THREE

THE SHEPHERD OF

Rest

"HE MAKES ME LIE DOWN IN GREEN PASTURES"

HER NAME IS SARA MARIE

With a mother too timid to shield her children and a father unafraid to rage at anyone in sight, Debbie spiraled downwards. It started with physical abuse, but before long Debbie's father added a layer of sexual abuse that eventually defined her childhood. She shared common beds with her four brothers and two sisters, and sexual dysfunction reigned.

"You're nothing but a whore," her father would yell. His prophetic words rang in her ears as Debbie became what he had called her. Within a week of turning eighteen, Debbie fled her home and began to lead a life no parents would want their daughters to live.

My soul finds rest in God alone; my salvation comes from him.
—Psalm 62:1

By day Debbie managed to work a full-time job with growth potential. After work, however, Debbie acted out the message her father had drummed into her head. Then, when she was

nineteen, on a snowy day in a shabby hospital that was ugly in every way, she allowed a doctor to kill her fourteen-week-old fetus. Of course she didn't think of her abortion as murder. She knew that what she had gotten rid of was certainly not a baby.

After the procedure, Debbie was sent to a room with several other young women. She lay down on a bed facing a window, rolled over on her side, and began to sob. By the time she left the hospital several hours later, it was through. She had stiffened herself against her actions and put them behind her.

I don't have to think about it, she thought, *don't have to raise it, don't have to deal with it every day.* She walked out of the hospital believing that the abortion wouldn't affect her career, her finances, her partying, and her nightly promiscuity.

For well over a decade, Debbie didn't worry about it. She did, however, drink herself into oblivion, get wasted on drugs, and indulge in too many sexual encounters to count. That was the legacy of her childhood: abuse taken and given. And pain, so much pain.

Like many others who hit bottom, Debbie somehow managed to make it to the top in her business life. But her professional success gave her little joy. She was tired of life, tired of herself.

Then, fourteen years after her abortion, the Shepherd put Debbie into the midst of one of the worst icy snowstorms in Minnesota history. As she slid down that treacherous road in her car, Debbie bargained with God. *I'll do anything, God, anything,* she promised. *Just get me to the next exit. If you get me out of this, I'll do whatever you want.*

God took her promise seriously. After making it home, she found her way into the safety of the Shepherd's arms and she committed her life to Him that same weekend. Ezekiel 11:19 reads, "I will give them a new heart and put a new spirit in

them; I will remove from them their heart of stone and give them a heart of flesh." And that is what God did for Debbie when she came crying and crawling back to the Shepherd, making deals, not knowing if He would take her seriously, for she had no idea that He would give her a new heart.

Debbie received her new heart that weekend, but only recently has she found total healing. She struggled for years until she participated in a Bible study at the Life Choice Pregnancy Center. Before starting the class, Debbie believed that she and God had dealt with all the issues involving her abortion. In fact, years earlier she had reunited with her boyfriend, Jack, not the father of the baby she had aborted, and became pregnant. She and Jack had married and their daughter, Sydney, was born.

Despite her husband and daughter, Debbie's pain and sorrow were never far from the surface. She knew that God had forgiven her of that sin and all the others. But could she ever forgive herself? She needed to accept that the price of her sins had already been paid in full; coming to the cross and forgiving herself could be her source of rest.

During the Bible study she started to remember a painful memory of something she had carried for a few weeks—a blob of tissue. Then she realized it hadn't been an it. *What she had done was sinful. She had aborted her baby.*

For twenty-five years her baby didn't have a name. Before she could forgive herself and grieve for her lost child, Debbie had one more step to take. She needed to acknowledge her baby, and that involved naming her.

Debbie had always known she would name her first

Give sorrow words; the grief that does not speak whispers the o'er-fraught heart and bids it break.
—William Shakespeare

daughter Sara Marie. When Jack came into the picture, though, he was adamant that his daughter would not be named Sara Marie. He never explained why, even

though Debbie tried to convince him on several occasions. So they named their daughter Sydney Alexandra, and that was that.

It had been years since Debbie had thought of the name *Sara Marie*, but as soon as the study leader recommended that she name her aborted child, Debbie understood. God had reserved that name for her first child.

Once her first baby had a name, Debbie could forgive herself. She wrote letters to Sara Marie and made her a quilt. Today Debbie doesn't feel any shame or guilt. The Shepherd has replaced her sorrow with joy, and she is looking forward to meeting one more person in heaven.

Working through the grief cycle brought Debbie healing and rest. With the Shepherd's help, she found a place in which to serve by helping other women understand that God would forgive them for their abortions. Grieving and healing didn't mean forgetting the abortion; it did mean integrating those experiences into her life and using them to help other women. Now she knows that the Shepherd can use every part of her life, even the worst parts.

In the Shepherd's perfect timing, after Debbie took the Bible study, ten-year-old Sydney approached her.

"Mommy, can I talk to you?"

"Sure, Sydney. What's up?"

"If someone I know wants to get an abortion, and she tells me, what should I say?"

Abortion? Debbie wondered. *Why is she asking me about abortion? What does she know?* Debbie still doesn't know why Sydney brought up the topic of abortion, but the Shepherd had already prepared her daughter's heart.

That day, twenty-five years after walking out of that ugly hospital, Debbie told her daughter the truth. Instead of revulsion or anger, Sydney responded with love.

"Can you forgive me, Sydney?"

"Of course I forgive you, Mommy."

Sydney then asked one more question.

"You mean I could have had a big sister?"

With a huge smile, Debbie answered, "Yes, her name is Sara Marie."

A crushing hurt comes to our heart and the sympathizing, scarred hand of Christ presses the wound; and just for a moment, the pain seems to intensify, . . . but finally the bleeding stops.
—Beth Moore

The eternal God is your refuge, and underneath are the everlasting arms.
—Deuteronomy 33:27

I HEARD THE VOICE OF JESUS SAY

HORATIUS BONAR

I heard the voice of Jesus say, "Come unto Me and rest;

Lay down, thou weary one, lay down Thy head upon My breast."

I came to Jesus as I was, weary and worn and sad;

I found in Him a resting place, and He has made me glad.

CHAPTER FOUR

THE SHEPHERD OF *Peace*

"HE LEADS ME BESIDE QUIET WATERS"

*Peace I leave with
you; my peace I
give you.*
—John 14:27

PERFECT PEACE

For twenty-year-old Cherie, life was great. Single, gorgeous, and living her dream as a singer in a traveling Top 40 band, she enjoyed the camaraderie of other band members. Until she met Lou, also a musician, she had no plans to change anything about her life.

"Tony Orlando," Cherie says simply, describing the dark-haired, mustached man who turned her head when he walked into the club where she was performing. Love at first sight is usually relegated to romantic comedies, but, Lou, wearing his black suit and red shirt, was not only the first "10" Cherie had ever met but was also someone she wanted to get to know.

During a break she introduced herself to Lou, and they talked as if they had always been friends. They agreed to join a group going out for a late-night meal, but when it was time to leave everyone else was too tired, so Lou and Cherie went by themselves.

I'm going to marry this guy, Cherie thought somewhere between dinner and good-bye. During the next eighteen months, she and Lou traded phone calls and visits. One night, while playing in a club in Kansas City, Cherie saw a patron get killed during a fight. Traumatized, all she wanted to do was quit the band, get off the road, and go home. She called Lou in Philadelphia who then invited her to be a vocalist in his band. With one failed marriage behind him, Lou didn't seem eager for a second walk down the aisle. Soon Cherie moved in with him. Lou continued to play with his band while working construction and Cherie began her career as a court reporter.

Thirteen years later, while working on a church construction site, Lou met Bruce, the pastor of the church. A lifelong friendship began. Pastor Bruce was nonjudgmental and seemed happy. Lou realized that although he and Cherie were in love and had a good life, they weren't happy in the same way Bruce seemed to be. There was a peace about Bruce that Lou wanted.

One evening Cherie walked in while Lou was on his knees. When she questioned what he was doing, Lou said that he was praying. After talking to Bruce, Lou had decided to become a Christian. Cherie, who until that moment had not felt a pull towards God, fell to her knees and also accepted the Lord. By June they were married and happier than they had ever been.

During the next six years, the couple grew closer to God and deeper in love. A series of events and job opportunities moved them from Philadelphia to Indiana. Then, in the midst of a terrible winter, the project Lou was working on wrapped up.

"Let's move to Florida," he suggested one day to his surprised wife.

Cherie was less than enthusiastic about the move, but she agreed to see what Tampa had to offer. While there, she interviewed with a court-reporting agency. Her twenty-year stint in the industry, coupled with the high demand for trained professionals, convinced her that getting a job in Tampa would be easy.

She prayed about the move for three weeks after she returned from Florida, only to find a closed door. "Maybe God isn't calling us to Tampa," Cherie mused after being told there were no jobs for her.

A business associate invited Lou to visit Naples. After his return, Cherie flew down and also became enchanted with the small southwest Florida community. Their home in Indiana sold quickly; the buyer wanted everything, including the furniture, pictures, and mementos. Cherie decided that with the money from the sale they could have fun starting over in Naples. With only a tiny trailer and a cat, they left for Florida.

Soon Lou and Cherie bought a waterfront condo and began decorating. Cherie sent out three resumes and received two job offers; that was all the confirmation she needed in order to know she was exactly where God wanted them to be. They found a home church, made friends, and began to create a new life.

Two months later, Cherie and a co-worker, Debbie, had to go to a certification class in Orlando, about a four-hour drive. On Friday, after her first day of classes, Cherie called home only to connect with the answering machine. Her worry about not talking with Lou vanished when she remembered that he was scheduled to fly that day.

Since he was a child, Lou had wanted to be a pilot. During the course of his life, he'd been in construction, owned a restaurant, and entertained through his music, but he loved flying the most. That day he was flying as a volunteer with a skywriting company.

As hours passed, Cherie became concerned when he didn't return her call at the hotel. "Something is wrong," Cherie finally told Debbie at six o'clock Saturday morning. "This is not like Lou. Something is very, very wrong."

Cherie called her office manager, Laura, at home one-half hour later and asked if she had heard of any airplane crashes. Laura's negative response did little to calm Cherie.

When Cherie and Debbie arrived at the convention center at 7:55 a.m., Cherie was more convinced than ever that Lou must have been in an accident. "I have to find out what's going on," she said as she hung up from calling Lou yet another time. Cherie then telephoned her ninety-year-old neighbor to see if she had any news.

"Oh, Cherie," she said. "The sheriff came looking for you at 2:00 this morning. Lou was in a crash. I'm sure he's fine, but you might want to call them at this number."

With a growing sense of alarm, Cherie called the sheriff, only to hear words she had somehow been expecting. The sheriff told her that Lou's plane had crashed on a major thoroughfare at 6:15 the previous evening. "I'm so sorry," he said as he gave her the victim's advocacy number. Cherie collapsed, and the next phase of her life began.

Only the Shepherd could have orchestrated the events that gave Cherie the peace she instinctively craved. Just when Cherie needed friends from her past, the Shepherd provided. On the way to Naples, Debbie drove her to St.

Petersburg where her former pastor from Indiana was now living. Together, they cried as Cherie prepared to face the inevitable challenges.

Cherie next called her father, then Lou's mother. Despite the reality that Lou—the love of her life, her best friend—had died, Cherie's inner peace never wavered. The thought that Lou, who had loved the Shepherd with all his mind, soul, and body was now in heaven, sustained her.

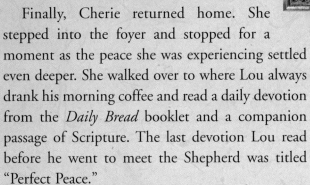

Finally, Cherie returned home. She stepped into the foyer and stopped for a moment as the peace she was experiencing settled even deeper. She walked over to where Lou always drank his morning coffee and read a daily devotion from the *Daily Bread* booklet and a companion passage of Scripture. The last devotion Lou read before he went to meet the Shepherd was titled "Perfect Peace."

Not only did the title give Cherie peace, but

also as she read the first few lines she knew that Lou's life, and the timing and circumstances of his death, were all within the Shepherd's control.

"Have you ever been in a situation where you thought you were about to die?" Lou had read those words and then, like the pilot quoted in the story, flew into a situation he had not anticipated. The pilot in the devotion knew he was about to die and took a few precious minutes to write his last will and testament. "There is peace, perfect peace," he wrote. "Life with Christ is the way to live. In this hour there is assurance —there is God underneath all the uncertainties of human existence. So I rest in God."

Memories of Lou flitted through Cherie's mind as she read those words. The Shepherd wrapped his arms around her as the force of the pilot's final words convicted her heart. "Trusting the Lord is indeed the best way to live. It is likewise the only way to die without fear."

God sweetens outward pain with inward peace.
—Thomas Watson

Without her knowledge, the Shepherd had prepared Cherie for being a young widow. She had sold not only her house but also all the personal belongings that would remind her daily of Lou. But the best preparation of all was the way in which Lou and Cherie had spent their last day together. The Wednesday before she had left they had laughed, kissed, and had what Cherie calls "a perfect day."

The Shepherd gave Cherie a perfect peace regarding the events surrounding Lou's death. Throughout the years that have followed, Cherie has learned that what the Italian poet, Dante Alighieri, said in the thirteenth century is still true: "In His will is our peace."

God cannot give us happiness and peace apart
from Himself, because it is not there.
—C. S. Lewis

Now may the Lord of peace himself give you
peace at all times and in every way.
—2 Thessalonians 3:16

LIKE A RIVER GLORIOUS

FRANCES R. HAVERGAL

Like a river glorious is God's perfect peace

Over all victorious, in its bright increase:

Perfect, yet it floweth fuller every day;

Perfect, yet it groweth deeper all the way.

CHAPTER FIVE

THE SHEPHERD OF

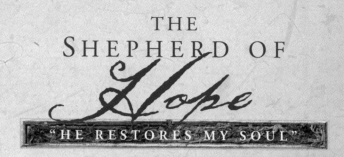

Hope

"HE RESTORES MY SOUL"

And our hope for you is firm, because we know that just as you share in our sufferings, so also you share in our comfort.

—2 Corinthians 1:7

THE REUNION NECKLACE

When Dianne was younger, her father, Ayward, was always there to comfort her. Whether she had a skinned knee or a lost kitten, he'd wipe her tears, and somehow Dianne knew things would be okay.

"Anything that can be fixed with money isn't too bad," he would remind Dianne when something terrible happened. Through the years, the combination of a hug, a handkerchief, just the right words, or sometimes even money helped her move past whatever had brought tears to her eyes.

Dianne was a young girl when her neighbor died in a farm tractor accident. *What if it had been my father who had died?* she wondered. The thought of living without her parents was unbearable, so she began to pray that they would live until the year 2000. That seemed like an eternity then, but Dianne felt that her prayers were being answered. Both her father and her mother, Jean, remained in good health apart from the occasional visit to the emergency room for a broken leg or an unusual case of shingles.

But everything changed during the summer of 1998. Ayward blacked out for no apparent reason, and his energy declined. He and Jean got a brief reprieve when the doctor said, "I don't know what you are worrying about, but there is nothing wrong with you. Go home and take it easy. You're just getting older."

When he didn't improve, Dianne believed whatever was wrong went beyond old age. She took her father to another doctor, who ordered tests on July 8, her father's seventy-fifth birthday. The startling diagnosis was stomach cancer.

"Can we stop by the store on the way home?" Her father's request startled Dianne, who had been deep in thought about her father's cancer.

"What do you want at the store that can't wait, Dad?"

"I lost my pocketknife and I need a new one."

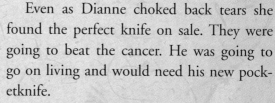

Even as Dianne choked back tears she found the perfect knife on sale. They were going to beat the cancer. He was going to go on living and would need his new pocketknife.

Twenty-two days later, after surgery, Ayward died. This time, however, there wasn't a big enough tissue box to comfort Dianne. Money could buy the best doctors, the newest treatments. But no amount of money could bring back her daddy. When Ayward took his last breath, a deep and devastating pain jockeyed for position with Dianne's memories for space in the empty piece of her heart left by her father's death.

How could she go on without his hugs, without benefit of his wisdom? She didn't want another bocce ball, shuffleboard, or dominoes partner. Who would share her quiet walks, bicycle rides, and good books?

At first, Dianne's tears were like ever-present intruders, forcefully making their presence known. They fell like a cold, steady rain. Some mornings, she'd have a secret cry in the shower so it wouldn't be so obvious to her husband and daughter. Dianne struggled daily to lock out the tears, yet she soon learned to welcome them as invited guests. They reminded her to be thankful that she had not only loved her father but had also been deeply loved.

During her journey through grief, Dianne never doubted the Shepherd's love. She did not need others to understand when she cried during a song or at the sight of her flowerbed full of weeds. The Shepherd understood that the song had been her father's favorite and that he was the one who had kept her garden weed-free. During all those times when she felt alone, the Shepherd was enough; he gave her hope.

Eventually the Shepherd brought hope to Dianne through His Word. She read the story of Abraham's death. When he died, he experienced a reunion with family and friends.

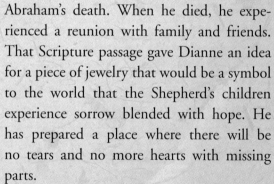

That Scripture passage gave Dianne an idea for a piece of jewelry that would be a symbol to the world that the Shepherd's children experience sorrow blended with hope. He has prepared a place where there will be no tears and no more hearts with missing parts.

Dianne is not an artist, but the Shepherd guided her as she designed what later became the Reunion Necklace. She took a heart-shaped drawing and cut out a small section. The cutout, later changed to a teardrop, symbolizes not only the shed tears but also the void left behind when a loved one dies. Thanks to a series of events orchestrated by the Shepherd, the product director from Cross Gifts saw Dianne's drawing and knew that the world needed this symbol of hope.

Alda, a writer familiar with the loss of a parent, wrote "The Reunion Heart" poem to accompany the sterling silver heart-shaped necklace. Her mother died when she was just twelve years old, so she and Dianne shared a pain that most of us know will come but try not to imagine. Alda, Dianne, and everyone involved with the project knew that what they created could be an important part of the healing process, something that would acknowledge the pain while emphasizing the hope that awaits those who will be reunited with loved ones in heaven.

It has been six years since Dianne's father arrived in heaven. Two years later, her mother joined him for their promised reunion. Dianne's necklace is

While we are mourning the loss of our friend, others are rejoicing to meet him behind the veil.
—John Taylor

a hopeful reminder that although she has cried, and will cry again, the Shepherd is well aware of each tear. In fact, Psalm 56:8 reminds all of us that the Shepherd keeps track of all our tears. On the day she re-joins her parents, Dianne likes to think

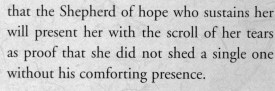

that the Shepherd of hope who sustains her will present her with the scroll of her tears as proof that she did not shed a single one without his comforting presence.

The cries of anguish, the deep-seated sobs,
and the shaking and heaving of the body of the
brokenhearted man are a testament to the fact that
the man who loves deeply will weep deeply.
—Zig Ziglar

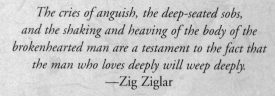

Those who sow in tears will reap with songs of joy.
—Psalm 126:5

THE REUNION HEART

ALDA MONTESCHIO

Since Heaven has become your home
I sometimes feel I'm so alone;
and though we now are far apart
you hold a big piece of my heart.

I never knew how much I'd grieve
when it was time for you to leave,
or just how much my heart would ache
from that one fragment you would take.

God lets the tender hole remain
to remind me we'll meet again,
and one day all the pain will cease
when He restores this missing piece.

He'll turn to joy my every tear,
and when I wear this necklace near
it will become my special way
to treasure our Reunion Day.

SWING LOW, SWEET CHARIOT

If you get there before I do,

Coming for to carry me home,

Tell all my friends I'm coming, too.

Coming for to carry me home.

CHAPTER SIX

THE
SHEPHERD WHO
Directs

**"HE GUIDES ME IN PATHS OF
RIGHTEOUSNESS FOR HIS NAME'S SAKE"**

MY TRUSTED FRIEND

As Joanne moved from home to home, during
her childhood years, Grandma Gladys became
her refuge. Although far from perfect and prone
to holding grudges, Gladys filled the deep empti-
ness inside the little girl. Most families she stayed
with while her mother worked didn't want to care
for a sick child, so they shuttled her to Grandma's
house. Sometimes Joanne even got sick just to be
with her grandmother.

After her mother remarried, Joanne visited
Gladys still. Years later as a young wife and mother,
Joanne still called on her grandmother even after

*For this God is our
God forever and
ever; he will be
our guide even
to the end.*
—Psalm 48:14

she moved into a nursing home. When the time came that Gladys needed someone to count on, Joanne wanted to be that someone.

Yet, as her grandmother's years in the nursing home increased, Joanne's resolve weakened and her visits grew fewer. *Look what happened the last time she needed me,* thought Joanne. *Even if I do drive forty-five minutes to see her I'll probably mess up again.*

One day Joanne got a call that her grandmother had pneumonia. It had been a year since her last visit to the nursing home, yet Joanne couldn't bring herself to go to her grandmother's bedside.

Joanne remembered that visit. She had received a similar call. She had thought that her love was strong enough to let her grandmother go. The day was hot and humid, the kind that no amount of air-conditioning relieves, when Joanne entered the room. Gladys lay in bed, curled up like a newborn baby. Her snow-colored hair fanned the pristine, white sheets. Her eyes were closed, her breathing labored. Nurses had attempted to make her comfortable, but she remained tense, her face drawn into a frown.

Leaning down to kiss Gladys's sunken cheeks and gently stroke her shriveled body, Joanne had whispered, "Grandma, Grandma, it's Joanne. Remember me?" Joanne thought of the times her grandmother had offered a soft lap to climb into, a bosom on which to lay her head. She had wanted to offer the same to Gladys, but it was too painful. The arms that had held her were black and blue from thrashing around to escape a worn-out body.

A nurse had pulled a chair next to the bed, and Joanne sat down.

"Grandma, it's Joanne. I'm here. Don't be afraid. I love you." Grandma hadn't opened her eyes, but she had seemed to relax a little. "Please Lord,"

Joanne had prayed silently, "don't let her suffer any-more. Help her go in peace."

Everything within Joanne had screamed for her to leave. This was too hard. She couldn't say good-bye to her grandmother—her best friend.

"Grandma, it's okay," she finally had said. "You can go now if you want. I love you." She had felt a growing calm as she repeated those words over and over. Her grandmother's hand had slackened, and the elderly woman lay perfectly still. Her breathing had become shallow. Then it happened. With a small cry, Joanne dropped her grandmother's hand and run from the room. An all-gripping panic had replaced her calm. All the way home, tears of anger at herself, mixed with those of sadness for her beloved grandmother, had blinded her.

Ashamed at not being able to stay with Gladys during such a time of deep need, Joanne had not visited her grandmother again. Yet the fact that her grandmother still lay confined within the prison of her body weighed heavily on Joanne's heart.

Now, a year later, another phone call had brought back all her feelings of self-disgust.

One day passed, then two. Gladys lingered almost as if she were waiting for her granddaughter to say good-bye. *I will not go*, Joanne argued with herself. *I cannot do this.*

On the third day she set out to do some errands. Suddenly, she realized that she was driving toward the nursing home. Her heart pounded. Indecisive thoughts mirrored her driving as she slowed down, sped up, then slowed down again.

"Lord, help me stay this time," Joanne prayed aloud. As if in answer, she focused on these words coming from the radio: "Good-bye to you, my trusted friend." Those few words directed Joanne to visit her grandmother again.

I can do this, Joanne thought seeing the raised bedside bars. A nurse sat nearby as Gladys thrashed back and forth. Joanne walked to her grandmother, took her hand, and tried to find the right words.

"May I put down the side so I can get closer to her?" she asked. In answer, the nurse put down the safety rail, pulled up a chair, and left the room. Before sitting down, Joanne leaned over and gently hugged and kissed Gladys, her trusted friend.

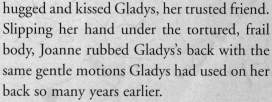

Slipping her hand under the tortured, frail body, Joanne rubbed Gladys's back with the same gentle motions Gladys had used on her back so many years earlier.

"Remember how you used to rub my back?" Joanne whispered. "Remember how we spooned in bed at night in the wintertime to keep warm?"

Her grandmother's grip relaxed a bit; her thrashing slowed.

"Remember how I used to come over to wash

your collection of salt and pepper shakers? How you helped the other kids and me put on circuses and plays in your backyard?"

As Gladys grew calmer, Joanne's panic of the previous year returned. Shutting her eyes tightly, she prayed for direction. The Shepherd answered her prayer. With a clarity of vision, she suddenly knew the source of her grandmother's agony—unresolved forgiveness.

"It's okay, Grandma," Joanne continued. "God forgives you. I know you forgive your sister, Mazie." One by one, Joanne listed people from the past who had hurt or been hurt by Gladys. "Grandma, you are forgiven. Everyone forgives you. Everyone accepts your forgiveness." Upon saying those words, Joanne felt the release. The calm she had felt briefly the year before returned. It was as though they both were suspended in time with no regrets and no fears.

Even when Gladys relaxed completely and

You will find, as you look back upon your life, that the moments . . . when you have really lived, are the moments when you have done things in a spirit of love.
—Henry Drummond

her breathing quieted, Joanne did not move away. They held hands in the silence. Some time passed before Joanne noticed music in the room. The voice she had heard on her car radio earlier sang, "Good-bye to you, my trusted friend."

A glowing smile replaced her grandmother's tortured grimace. Her breathing, once labored, grew slow and easy.

"Say hello to Grandpa for me," Joanne whispered as she kissed Gladys good-bye.

Joanne walked to her car and within minutes of starting home the comforting song filled the car and her heart. "Good-bye to you, my trusted friend."

Gladys, still smiling, died two hours after Joanne arrived home. Together she and her trusted friend had walked together through the valley of the shadow of death, directed by the Shepherd.

In helping others, we shall help ourselves,
for whatever good we give out completes
the circle and comes back to us.
—Flora Edwards

You guide me with your counsel, and
afterward you will take me into glory.
—Psalm 73:24

GOD LEADS US ALONG

George A. Young

Some through the waters, some through the flood,

Some through the fire, but all through the blood;

Some through great sorrow, but God gives a song,

In the night season and all the day long.

CHAPTER SEVEN

THE
SHEPHERD OF
Patience

"EVEN THOUGH I WALK THROUGH THE VALLEY OF THE SHADOW OF DEATH"

TEACH US TO PRAY

The wife of a Foreign Service officer, Elaine lived in many countries over the years. Inquisitive and friendly, she built many friendships, only to leave those friends behind whenever her husband, Don, received a new posting. Still, some friends made an impression on her heart, and Elaine made it a point to keep in contact with them. Although considerably younger than Elaine, Pam was one of those friends.

Larry, Pam's husband, had served with Don in Indonesia. When communists there tried to take over, Elaine and Pam and their children were

God will fulfill all of His promises to those who wait patiently.
—Hebrews 10:36
(author paraphrase)

evacuated to the Philippines. The two women supported each other through difficult times. Now Pam needed support again.

Inoperable. That's how doctors described Larry's cancer. Elaine and her daughter, Vicki, were crushed to read Pam's note bearing such devastating news. They decided that God couldn't want Larry, a great guy with such young children, to die, so they decided to do something about it. The two women made a pact that they would pray for him every day and fast on Thursday, until Larry was restored to health.

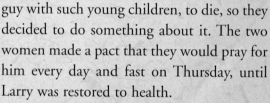

Elaine and Vicki's close proximity made it easier for them to keep their vow. Vicki, her husband, John, and little Andrea had moved back in with Elaine and Don when John couldn't find work. When Vicki married John she thought he was a Christian, but she soon found out he wasn't. When John saw his wife and mother-in-law so eager and sure that God would answer their prayers, he pledged, "If Larry is healed, I'll become a Christian." This promise fueled their passion, and they prayed more earnestly.

After a few weeks of praying, Elaine knew exactly the words of encouragement she would write to Pam: "Hang in there. Vicki and I are praying and fasting for Larry, and I have assurance that he will be healed." Before she wrote the letter, however, she received another note. Larry had died. Pam was a widow with three small children.

Elaine and Vicki wept. They were not only devastated for Pam but wondered about how the news would affect John. Would he reject God, using Larry's death as proof that Christianity wasn't true?

Elaine's faith was shaken. *Didn't God hear our prayers?* she wondered. *Did we pray the wrong way? Should we have fasted a different way?* Obviously something was amiss.

In Elaine's confusion, she cried out, and the

Shepherd answered in a way she never could have predicted. She began to search the Bible for everything she could discover about prayer. For weeks, she took notes on all the times people in the Bible prayed, about what Jesus and Paul said about prayer, and how the Old Testament prophets prayed. Insight after insight kept her riveted to the written Word as she found things she'd never heard from a pulpit.

Elaine's patience, a gift from the Shepherd, paid off in two different ways. She came to terms with Larry's death and had enough notes to write a Bible study. A new organization for women had sprung up, and it needed Bible studies that could be used in home study groups. She organized her material, wrote a Bible study with added study questions, revised and proofed everything, and sent off the manuscript.

Eventually the editor wrote back saying that they liked the study but that the women in the organiza-

Only with winter-patience can we bring the deep-desired, long-awaited spring.
—Anne Morrow Lindbergh

tion were still too young in the Lord to use it. They asked if they could hold onto the manuscript for a while. Since Elaine had written it for this specific group, she told the editors to contact her when they were ready to publish her manuscript.

About two years later, the editor wrote to Elaine that they wanted to use her material for a Bible study, but that they'd started revising the deeper studies using a different format. Would she allow them to revise it and add an "extra credit" passage at the end of each chapter? Elaine agreed, and within a few months she received a copy of her Bible study, *Teach Us to Pray*.

Several years later, a Spanish-language edition appeared in her mailbox. As she flipped through its pages, she marveled that women from all over Latin America, southwestern United States, and many other places around the world were being

drawn closer to God because of that Bible study. The Shepherd was using her patience, formed by grief, in ways she never could have predicted.

About ten years later, Elaine attended a large conference sponsored by the women's group. On the book table were all the Bible studies and other books the organization had published. In front of each book was a chart showing the translations that now existed for each. *Teach Us to Pray* had been translated into fourteen languages, not only such common ones as French and German, but also the languages of Urdu and Swahili!

When Elaine reflects on Larry's death, she can't help but be astonished at all that the Shepherd has accomplished as a result. Pam eventually married another kind, supportive man who loves her children as his own.

What happened to John? Despite Larry's death,

or rather because of it, the Shepherd moved in John's heart. "If two women can be so earnest about praying for a sick person, so sure that he's being healed, then that's enough for me," he said. But that was just the beginning of how Elaine's prayers transformed John's life.

John went to seminary, became a pastor, planted a church, took Vicki and their children to be missionaries to Guatemala, and pastored other churches in America. For many years, John has taken an annual work team of either builders or doctors and nurses to Honduras in conjunction with a local church there.

French philosopher and social reformer Jean Jacques Rousseau wrote, "Patience is bitter, but its fruit is sweet." Larry's death was a bitter pill for Elaine to swallow, but the fruit of her patience is sweet and still bearing fruit around the world. Through Larry's death Elaine learned that the Shepherd is always perfect and will always use what is painful to us for His good purposes. We just need to be patient.

> *More things are wrought by prayer*
> *than the world dreams of.*
> —Alfred, Lord Tennyson

> *Wait for the LORD; be strong and take*
> *heart and wait for the LORD.*
> —Psalm 27:14

SWEET HOUR OF PRAYER

William Walford

Sweet hour of prayer! sweet hour of prayer!

That calls me from a world of care,

And bids me at my Father's throne

Make all my wants and wishes known.

In seasons of distress and grief,

My soul has often found relief,

And oft escaped the tempter's snare

By thy return, sweet hour of prayer!

CHAPTER EIGHT

THE SHEPHERD OF

Courage

"I WILL FEAR NO EVIL"

Be strong and take heart, all you who hope in the LORD.
—Psalm 31:24

THIRTEEN DIAMONDS

Learning that she was pregnant with her second child should have been a reason for celebration. But Nancy, the mother of a five-year-old son who had several learning disabilities, was apprehensive.

"I'm afraid I won't have enough energy to take care of Nick and a newborn," Nancy explained to her husband, Ron.

"You'll do great, Honey," he encouraged, thrilled that a second child was coming.

As Nancy repeated the familiar cycle of required medical appointments, the doctor assured her that everything was fine. "There's nothing to worry about," he said. "However, since you'll be thirty-five when the baby is born, we just want to do an ultrasound. More often than not age isn't a problem, but there is a higher chance of a baby with birth defects."

Telling Nancy not to worry was like telling someone who has heard a sound in the middle of the night it's probably not a burglar. Nancy worried until the day of her ultrasound appointment.

As the aid squirted the cold sonogram gel on her expanding belly, Nancy tried to find a comfortable spot on the hard examination table. One technician slid the scope over her stomach while the other one watched the monitor.

Just a routine exam, Nancy thought as she looked at the woman watching the monitor. *It will be fine.*

Nancy continued watching. Within minutes, the woman's expression changed. Her eyes widened, and her hands flew involuntarily to her mouth as she made a sad, squeaking sound.

"What's wrong?" Nancy asked. When no one answered, she sat up and repeated her question.

"I'm sorry," whispered the technician, trying to compose herself as she scurried toward the door.

Nancy watched with mounting fear as the second technician left the room. Left alone, she slid off the table and went to look at the image still on the screen. All she saw was what looked like a blurry negative of a skinny baby. "I think we're in trouble," she said aloud looking down and rubbing her stomach.

After further testing, Nancy and Ron listened to the doctor who, with all the warmth of someone reading a textbook, stated, "Trisomy 18 is a genetic disorder that always involves profound mental retardation and severe disfigurements."

Barely able to comprehend this news, Nancy

next heard the words that still live inside a tiny, zipped pocket of her heart.

"Your baby's condition is usually incompatible with life. Most women in your position, in order to spare themselves unnecessary anguish, just get an abortion. We can schedule yours for tomorrow morning."

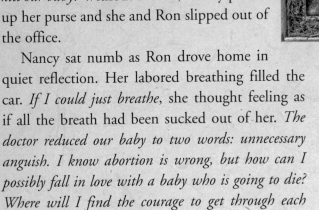

An abortion? She thought. *How could I kill our baby?* Without a word, Nancy picked up her purse and she and Ron slipped out of the office.

Nancy sat numb as Ron drove home in quiet reflection. Her labored breathing filled the car. *If I could just breathe*, she thought feeling as if all the breath had been sucked out of her. *The doctor reduced our baby to two words: unnecessary anguish. I know abortion is wrong, but how can I possibly fall in love with a baby who is going to die? Where will I find the courage to get through each day?*

That evening as Nancy prayed she reflected on the courage required for Jesus to do his Father's will. *He could have chosen to avoid the horrific agony of the cross. What if He had taken the easy way out?* After several agonizing hours Nancy knew what she had to do.

Nancy, like countless women who choose life for their babies, took an incredibly courageous step. She still feared, but the Shepherd, Who has experienced every emotion we will ever have, gave her the courage to make the right choice.

"I offer my sorrow to you as a gift," she prayed when she realized that the value of Jesus' gift was measured by the greatness of his suffering. "I will not abort this child," she continued. "I choose to love this baby with all my heart."

In faith, she moved her hands as she caressed her stomach. In faith, she moved her lips as she mouthed the words, "I love you." No sound came out. She kept repeating the phrase until her brain found the secret passageway to her heart and she was free to taste the bittersweet tears of loving a child who might never say, "I love you."

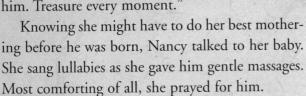

As her pregnancy progressed, whenever Nancy's courage failed she remembered her mother's words: "Try not to think about the future. Your baby is alive today; be alive with him. Treasure every moment."

Knowing she might have to do her best mothering before he was born, Nancy talked to her baby. She sang lullabies as she gave him gentle massages. Most comforting of all, she prayed for him.

Four months later, Nancy and Ron met little Timmy, face-to-face. The nurse covered his fragile, twenty-ounce body with a soft, blue blanket and matching cap. His heart monitor beeped an unsteady greeting.

His little rosebud-shaped mouth, an oasis of perfection, surprised Nancy. She and Ron held their emotions in check, knowing they had to pour 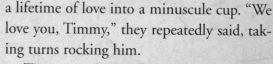 a lifetime of love into a minuscule cup. "We love you, Timmy," they repeatedly said, taking turns rocking him.

Timmy never opened his eyes. His heartbeat became slower and slower, then stopped. As the couple held their son, they released him to his heavenly Father. "Lord, here is our son," they prayed. "Thank you for the gift of his precious life and for the privilege of being his parents. We release him into your healing arms."

A few days after Timmy went home to be with the Shepherd, her days filled with tears but not regret, Nancy contacted a jeweler. She drew a picture of a ring's design and the jeweler worked late into the night to complete it.

Today, on her baby finger Nancy wears a

reminder of her son. The ring has two curved bands of gold. The longer one symbolizes her husband's arm; the smaller band represents hers. Their symbolic arms hold a small, lavender alexandrite (Timmy's birthstone). Surrounding the stone are thirteen tiny diamonds—one precious jewel for each minute that Timmy was alive.

Nancy doesn't need a ring to remind her of the son she will meet in heaven, nor does she need a ring to remind her of the Shepherd's love. Timmy, and the Shepherd, both live in her heart, just as the ring remains on her finger.

Courage is not the towering oak that sees storms come and go; it is the fragile blossom that opens in the snow.
—Alice Mackenzie Swaim

> *To have courage for whatever comes in life—everything lies in that.*
> —Mother Teresa

> *God has said, "Never will I leave you; never will I forsake you." So we say with confidence, "The Lord is my helper; I will not be afraid.*
> —Hebrews 13:5, 6

I MUST TELL JESUS

Elisha A. Hoffman

I must tell Jesus all of my trials;

I cannot bear these burdens alone;

In my distress He kindly will help me;

He ever loves and cares for His own.

I must tell Jesus! I must tell Jesus!

I cannot bear my burdens alone;

I must tell Jesus! I must tell Jesus!

Jesus can help me, Jesus alone.

CHAPTER NINE

THE SHEPHERD OF

Friends

"FOR YOU ARE WITH ME"

LUNCHPAIL FRIENDS

Four-year-old Bruce was used to strangers. It seemed as if every few days another family moved into his mother's mobile home park in upstate New York. Inquisitive and spunky, Bruce would ask everyone he didn't know, "Hey, you moving in here?"

"Hey, Mister," he asked one day, "you moving in here?"

"Yeah," answered sixteen-year-old Bill, who wasn't used to being called *Mister*. "We live here now."

Despite their huge age difference, the two became fast friends. It's still a mystery why Bill

A friend loves at all times, and a brother is born for adversity.

—Proverbs 17:17

befriended a boy just entering kindergarten, but Bruce's question prompted a lasting friendship.

Besides the usual things boys do—talk, play sports, get into innocent trouble—after awhile the two had something else in common. Seemingly overnight, Bruce's sister, Ruth, blossomed into more than a big sister and the landlord's child. Bill and Ruth became sweethearts and dated during all four years of his navy service and her high school days. Whenever his hero came home on leave, Bruce managed to tag along with the couple and even spend time alone with Bill.

After their marriage, Bill and Ruth worked hard to build a trailer court in upstate New York. Eventually Ruth's family, including Bruce, moved to Virginia Beach, Virginia. Bill and Ruth decided to follow suit, selling the business and moving into her mother's trailer court.

Most people in this area either worked for the

U.S. Navy or Norfolk Southern Railroad. Having served his time in the military, Bill donned a railroad conductor's hat and toted his plastic lunchpail to work every day. Besides his meal he carried his railroad key, cigarettes, lighter, and even toilet tissue. Because he came from up north, the other workers called him "Mr. Yankee," and Bill scratched that name on the end of his lunchpail. Over the years it became bent and dirty, and a strong string replaced its broken handle, but Bill never retired his treasure.

In 1984, Bill fell from the top of a moving railroad car and lost both legs. Bruce and Ruth arrived at the hospital simultaneously. They hugged each other and wondered about Bill's future. He was in the trauma unit for three months and on the regular floor for another month. After he came home, strange things began to happen. His hands would fly all over and he had trouble sit-

ting on the commode. He'd yell out in the middle of the night. He began to curse more and yell at Ruth for no reason. At first people thought it was caused by the loss of his legs and his withdrawal from all the medication he had been receiving. Eventually the doctors diagnosed Bill with Huntington's, a rare neurological disease.

As the years passed, Bruce visited Bill more than any other person. Now married with children of his own, Bruce never stopped befriending Bill. He would give him a shave, cut his hair, and even feed him. Both men, more like brothers than friends, teased and joked with each other and shared memories.

In 1995 Bill went home to heaven and Ruth and Bruce comforted each other. Now when Bruce came to visit his big sister each week, he would always ask, "Need anything done, Ru-fer?" He'd cut the grass or chop wood, whatever needed doing. Ruth would thank him with a good home-cooked meal.

One day Ruth asked Bruce, "Do you want any of Bill's stuff, something to remember him by?"

After a minute or two he replied, "Yeah, I'd like his lunchpail."

"Why in the world would you want that dirty, coal-dusted, battered lunchpail?"

With a shrug and a smile, Bruce grabbed the memento and began using it every day. He drove his own logging truck, and each morning when he slid onto the front seat Bill's lunchpail was right there beside him. And like Bill, he placed anything and everything he might need in it. He never went anywhere without it. When he came to visit his sister he would walk in swinging the lunchpail, grin and say, "Hi Ru-fer!"

Eleven years after his friend died, Bruce was diagnosed with lung cancer. Long divorced, he moved into Ruth's home. Bruce and Ruth both knew that death meant being reunited with Bill, but they still prayed for more time together. The doctors told Bruce that if he wanted a year more of life he'd have to receive a series of chemotherapy treatments, so Ruth and Bruce talked often on the way to the hospital for each round of chemo, and the lunchpail made every trip.

Before he died, Bruce decided to be cremated. He picked out the funeral home, talked about a family gathering after the funeral, and asked to be buried in the Shenandoah Mountains. He told Ruth all she needed to know, but when the time finally came, his big sister had a difficult time.

"This is too hard," Ruth cried out in the car on the day she went to pick up Bruce's remains. "How can I let him go? He's more than my brother, he's my best friend." Ruth prayed to the Shepherd about the impossible good-bye, and the Shepherd answered.

The woman handling the transaction asked if Ruth would like to buy a special container for her brother's ashes. Ruth stood for a moment, realizing that Bruce

Friendships begin because, even without words, we understand how someone feels.
—Joan Walsh Anglund

had not told her what he wanted. She looked at the variety of urns, but nothing seemed right.

"Please, Lord, help me decide," she prayed silently to the Shepherd. Suddenly she thought of the perfect container.

"Could I bury him in a lunchpail?"

The flustered woman thought about it for a moment before answering. "We've never had anyone use a lunchpail before, but I don't see why not."

During the day of the memorial service, everyone celebrated Bruce's life. Ruth created a tribute to her brother that included his logging hat, photographs of him in military school, and—right in the middle—she placed the plastic lunchpail. After the celebration, a few people carried Bruce's ashes to a perfect spot on the side of the mountain he loved so much. After Bruce's friends dug a deep hole, Ruth prayed and lowered the plastic lunchpail. Finally they rolled a large stone over the hole and walked back down the mountain.

"I still miss my two best friends and always will," says Ruth. "I know I'll see them one day. I can almost see that old lunchpail right beside them up in heaven." She takes comfort in knowing that they are together with the Shepherd—the best friend of all.

Don't be dismayed at good-byes. A farewell is necessary before you can meet again. And meeting again, after moments or lifetimes, is certain for those who are friends.
—Richard Bach

Though he brings grief, he will show compassion, so great is his unfailing love.
—Lamentations 3:32

BLEST BE THE TIE

JOHN FAWCETT

Blest be the tie that binds

Our hearts in Christian love;

The fellowship of kindred minds

Is like to that above.

CHAPTER TEN

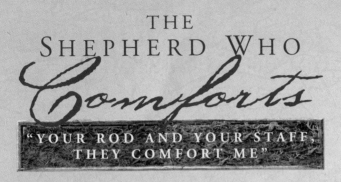

THE
SHEPHERD WHO
Comforts

"YOUR ROD AND YOUR STAFF, THEY COMFORT ME"

DOOPTY-DOOP LOVE

To ten-year-old Blair, her father, Bob, was that big strong man every little girl looks up to. He also could be counted on to provide fun and activities. They held picnics every Labor Day, and every neighbor came. Bob always organized the kids' games for that day. He orchestrated scavenger hunts, three-legged races, and obstacle courses for bike riders—and made sure everyone received a prize. Most importantly, he made sure everyone laughed.

Work-related travels gradually kept him away from his family for longer periods of time and she discovered what it meant for a father to have an

Comfort, comfort my people, says your God.
—Isaiah 40:1

affair. Bob's drinking turned into alcoholism, and at age fourteen, Blair drank her first beer, and, on that same day, her father let her practice driving.

"Don't tell your mother," Bob reminded, fully aware that sparks would fly if his wife found out. She never did. There were many don't-tell-your-mother moments before she went away to college.

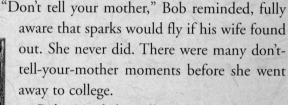

Bob visited the college she attended several times and called now and then. And every time he still laughed—an infectious laugh when he was having a good day and a nervous laugh on the not so good ones.

Eventually her parents divorced and Blair moved to the other side of the country after graduation. She kept in close contact with her mother and saw her father from time to time. When Blair announced she was getting married, Bob sobered up just before the wedding.

When Blair turned thirty-two, her father was diagnosed with a disease that robbed him of his ability to use his eyes, facial muscles, and eventually to swallow. Her sister, Kate, worked with the insurance and social service agencies, while her brother, Jim, began untangling a lifetime of bad financial habits that included never balancing a checkbook. Blair's job was to learn all she could about the disease.

Eventually, she and her family moved back to Minnesota, where she again connected with her father during visits to the nursing home in which he lived.

They shared more meaningful conversations than they'd ever had, and those conversations always led to laughter as they recalled fun times in the neighborhood, quirky things in life, and some of their more tender moments.

One beautiful afternoon shortly before he died, Blair traveled to the nursing home with her four- and six-year-old daughters. She wheeled her father out to the patio and gave him a chocolate milkshake. As they watched the girls play, she asked, "Dad, remember when I was that age? You'd tuck me in at night, and you'd have all my stuffed animals join me one at a time."

A single sunbeam is enough to drive away many shadows.
—St. Francis of Assisi

She smiled, remembering the way he had bounced each one up the bed, making a little "humdeedoe, doopty-doop" sound right next to her little face as each animal in its own voice would plead homelessness and ask if it could sleep on her bed that night. She'd giggle and find a square inch or two for each to snuggle into. By the time he was done, she hardly had room to turn over or move, but she didn't care. She was cozy in her animal fortress. Bob would then kiss her forehead, say "Goodnight Punkin" and head down the hall.

"Guess what?" Blair continued, "I do it with my girls now. They love it. They say, 'Mom, can you do the Doopty-Doop tonight?' and we do it as often as we can."

A tear dripped down Bob's cheek as he sipped his

milkshake. Then, in as clear a voice as Blair had heard in months, he said, "I'll never forget."

Blair fought back tears realizing that he also shared her childhood remembrance. Taking a deep breath, she turned to watch her daughters and laugh at their antics.

During her father's memorial service, Blair shared the Doopty-Doop story. She began to cry as she recounted these precious memories. The crowd waited for her to regain her composure and continue her story. Glancing at her notes, she realized she had lost her place.

"Excuse me a moment," she apologized, "I can't see."

Kate, in the spirit of their father and his humor, piped up from the front row, "Need my glasses?" Everyone laughed as their shared memories of Bob and his humor continued to comfort them.

Since her father's death, Blair has found comfort in doing the Doopty-Doop with her daughters more often. Some nights, as she makes the "humdeedoe, doopty-doop" sound right next to their little faces, she remembers her father sitting  in his wheelchair on the nursing home's patio. She feels that he has never forgotten and that each time they play Doopty-Doop, her father is laughing right along with them.

The late Bob Hope said, "I have seen what a laugh can do. It can transform almost unbearable tears into something bearable, even hopeful." Now almost forty, Blair has seen how through laughter the Shepherd can comfort those who thought they would never laugh again. She is grateful for her father's legacy of silly games and infectious laughter. They, along with the Shepherd, will continue to comfort her forever.

*Laughter gives us distance. It allows us to step back
from an event, deal with it and then move on.*
—Bob Newhart

*He will yet fill your mouth with laughter
and your lips with shouts of joy.*
—Job 8:21

UNDER HIS WINGS

William O. Cushing

Under His wings, what a refuge in sorrow!

How the heart yearningly turns to His rest!

Often when earth has no balm for my healing,

There I find comfort, and there I am blessed.

CHAPTER ELEVEN

THE SHEPHERD OF *Protection*

"YOU PREPARE A TABLE BEFORE ME IN THE PRESENCE OF MY ENEMIES"

MOMENTS OF CHOICE

There was no reason for Ralph to die that September evening. It wasn't a robbery, though of course that wouldn't have made Connie feel any better about her son's death. On the night of Ralph's murder, four boys raised in one of the wealthiest towns in the area took turns drinking, driving, and randomly shooting two .22-caliber rifles at joggers and passersby. They also fired into a home and a convenience store. At 1:30 a.m., Ralph locked up the restaurant where he worked. Ten minutes later as he rode his bicycle home, a single bullet struck the back of his head.

The teenagers had nothing against their vic-

God will take care of you.
—Psalm 27:10

tims. In fact, they didn't even know Ralph or the soldier they wounded during their spree.

All that year, Connie had been praying earnestly and faithfully for Ralph and his twin brother, Quentin. After Connie and her husband, Ed, returned from a four-month mission trip to the Cook Islands, Ralph began to telephone them more frequently. During each call, Ralph shared more and more about things in his life, including the time he spent in church with his friend, Chuck, and that he had become a Christian. Connie was pleased because Ralph had never willingly gone to church unless she had invited him. She knew that God was answering her prayers for Ralph.

Later that year, Ed traveled to Israel, but this time Connie stayed home. While Ed was away, Ralph invited Connie to join him on two different day trips. During both adventures, they talked virtually non stop as they drove through the mountains.

They discussed everything from the trivial to the serious. Those long days were a gift from God showing her that Ralph had matured and was growing in ways she was praying for.

Now Ralph was dead, and Connie wrestled with difficult issues. During the next few months, she questioned the senselessness of Ralph's death. "God, I trusted you," she cried, grieving. "You know I prayed for him every day. I prayed protection from the enemy every day."

As her tears dried she sensed the Shepherd's answer. "How would you feel if you had not prayed?"

Connie realized then that she would have felt enormous guilt, as if his death were her fault because she had not covered him in prayer. Knowing that she couldn't have protected Ralph from every earthly harm, Connie continued to pray and cry out for understanding. Eventually she learned that one of the medical technicians on the rescue ambulance was an unscheduled replacement that night. As they passed Ralph, something by the road caught his eye. Before the ambulance reached the next traffic light, he said, "I think we'd better turn around and go back. I think I saw someone in the ditch back there."

So, within a few minutes of being shot, Ralph received care. Because of the Shepherd's protection, Ralph had not lain in the ditch for hours, leaving his family to wonder how things might have been if help had gotten there sooner. "Before his head even touched the ground, Connie said, "the Shepherd had Ralph in his arms; He had protected Ralph from an eternity apart from Him."

As much as Connie's heart broke because of her son's murder, she knew that she'd rather be the mother of the victim than the mother of the murderer. Still, her grief grew as she pondered the circumstances surrounding the random choice of her son's death.

One afternoon, Connie remembered something Ralph had shared during one of their day trips. Seemingly out of context with the current conversation, Ralph had said, "Mom, I don't mind dying; it's not the dying. I just want my life to have meant something." At the time Connie had not thought about his comment, but in hindsight she wondered, *did Ralph have a premonition of his impending death?* As she tried to make sense of the situation, Connie shared Ralph's comment with family members, including her daughter, Nicole, who was also questioning why Ralph had died. Through her sobs, Nicole had heard the Shepherd's quiet assurance: "This will not be in vain."

That promise galvanized Nicole to establish a powerful ministry, which includes a presentation titled "One Family, One Life, One Night— Moments of Choice." The presentation begins

"To live is to suffer; to survive is to find meaning in suffering."
—Viktor Frankel

with sequential pictures of Ralph from infancy in Connie's arms through his midthirties. Gunshots sound rhythmically as a popular song about life and death plays in the background. After the opening, Nicole walks onto the stage.

The hour-long program gives Nicole an opportunity to help students consider their choices before they lead to a tragedy. At one point toward the end, Nicole reveals that the man on the screen is her brother. Each time, the audience gasps as they listen to someone who has had to live with the consequences thrust on her after four young men made terrible choices. In this way, Ralph's life has made a tremendous impact on many young people.

Connie's faith continued to grow stronger throughout the funeral and subsequent arrests, trials, and convictions of the four men involved in the shooting. Each day, she prayed, "God, I don't understand you, but I really do trust you." That trust gave her time to listen as the Shepherd unfolded many answers into her receptive heart and mind.

"Not a day passes that I don't miss Ralph," Connie says. "But thanks to the Shepherd's protection, I know that I will see him in heaven for eternity."

You gain strength, courage and confidence by every experience in which you really stop to look fear in the face. You are able to say to yourself, "I have lived through this horror. I can take the next thing that comes along."
—Eleanor Roosevelt

The LORD will keep you from all harm—he will watch over your life; the LORD will watch over your coming and going both now and forever more.
—Psalm 121: 7, 8

O GOD, OUR HELP IN AGES PAST

ISAAC WATTS

O God, our help in ages past,

Our hope for years to come,

Our shelter from the stormy blast,

And our eternal home.

CHAPTER TWELVE

THE SHEPHERD WHO *Heals*

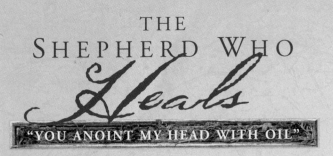

"YOU ANOINT MY HEAD WITH OIL"

ONLY ONE LIFE

"He's not going to die," declared my sister-in-law Christina. "God is going to heal Merrill." So intent was Christina in her belief that not even her husband's yellowed skin and emaciated frame swayed her from telling everyone that he would get better. Despite his drug-induced psychosis and failing vital signs, Christina anticipated my brother's imminent move from intensive care to a regular room. She was convinced that Merrill would walk out of the hospital, alive and healthy. In contrast, my sister, Patricia, an emergency room nurse, told us what to expect. The prognosis was grim. Barring a miracle, Merrill would not improve this time as he had countless times before.

. . . For the LORD comforts his people and will have compassion on his afflicted ones.
—Isaiah 49:13

Grieving doesn't always begin with death. For those who love someone who has a devastating terminal illness, the grieving process begins as the likelihood of survival diminishes. Denial is one stage of grief, and Christina was entrenching herself in denial.

As Merrill's condition worsened, Christina's resolve strengthened. She believed that her husband—the father of their seven-year-old son—was not going to die. Together they had served in ministry and built a thriving church. "There is so much left for Merrill to do," she exclaimed. "How could God not heal such a faithful man?"

From around the country his seven siblings arrived to say good-bye to him. With our parents, spouses, and various children, we crowded into the intensive care unit's waiting room. We took turns standing by Merrill's bedside, amazed that his wasted body still functioned.

One morning before going to the hospital my oldest brother, Kevin, and his wife, Karen talked about Christina's denial.

"Kevin, I'm worried," said Karen. "I don't think Merrill is going to make it. I'm afraid Christina will regret not saying good-bye to Merrill before he dies." She also feared that seven-year-old David would not be able to say farewell to his father, either.

"Karen, God showed me that Merrill will be going to heaven soon," Kevin replied as they left for the hospital. He then described a dream he'd had a few days earlier. In his dream, Kevin saw a box in heaven engraved with Merrill's name and filled to the brim with golden coins. On these coins were noted the names of people Merrill had led to the Lord, deeds he had done in the name of Jesus, people he had helped, and songs he had written.

"As I stepped closer and peered inside," Kevin

continued, "I saw that the box was so filled that not even one more coin could be placed inside. I believe that my dream means that because Merrill's treasure box is full, Merrill's job on earth is complete. God wants him home."

When they reached the hospital, Karen and Kevin walked with Christina and David into the chapel. "Christina, Merrill is tired," said Karen. "You need to release him."

"It's not time," Christina cried, tears streaming. "God's going to heal Merrill."

"God heals in different ways," explained Kevin. "Merrill has done more for God in the twenty or so years since he began living for Jesus than most of us do in our entire lives. God will heal Merrill, but that healing won't be on earth. You and David need to tell him good-bye. Tell him it's okay to go home to heaven."

All four of them entered Merrill's room, and Kevin moved a chair next to the bed. David, who

God is in the details.
—Ludwig Mies van der Rohe

had often imitated Merrill by preaching into a hairbrush, stood on the chair, leaned over his daddy, and grabbed his hand. "Daddy, I love you," he said. "But if you want to go and be with Jesus, if you're tired of being sick, it's okay." With great seriousness, and maturity far beyond his years, David gave his beloved father permission to leave.

While Karen and Kevin comforted David, Christina then embraced the man she had loved in sickness and in health. "You've been such a good husband, Merrill," she said. "I don't want you to die. I want God to heal you. I love you, but if God says you're done here on earth, I understand."

Merrill, who had often been incoherent in recent days, for a brief time understood when it mattered the most. He smiled broadly and said, "Okay, okay."

Christina hugged David as Merrill fell asleep.

"He'll always be with us, Honey," she explained to David. "Always."

The Shepherd graciously allowed our family to see that a simple verse became the cornerstone of Merrill's life. After becoming a Christian Kevin attached a plaque to a kitchen cabinet door. He decided that even if no one wanted to talk about Christ they could at least read about him each morning as they reached for a drinking glass. The words on the plaque cited the last words of the missionary David Livingstone, "Only one life twill soon be past. Only what's done for Christ will last."

Soon after Christina and David told Merrill good-bye, Kevin, who had led Merrill to the Lord twenty-two years earlier, stood by his side. Suddenly, a strong voice replacing his frail whisper, Merrill stated, "Only one life twill soon be past. Only what's done for Christ will last."

Certainly the Shepherd of healing greeted

Merrill as he entered heaven. Perhaps he even ushered Merrill to a treasure box filled with coins, signifying that Merrill had indeed accomplished much for Christ.

It didn't happen overnight, but their unselfish acts of giving Merrill permission to die began the healing process for Christina and David. With Kevin and Karen's help, the Shepherd walked Christina and David through denial, anger, bargaining, depression, and into acceptance. One day He'll walk each of them into heaven to join Merrill. Meanwhile, they know that only what's done for Christ will last.

Of one thing I am certain, the body is not the measure of healing, peace is the measure.
—George Melton

He forgives all my sins and heals all my diseases . . .
—Psalm 103:3

HAVE THINE OWN WAY, LORD

Adelaide A. Pollard

Have Thine own way, Lord! Have Thine own way!

Wounded and weary, help me, I pray!

Power, all power, surely is Thine!

Touch me and heal me, Savior divine!

CHAPTER THIRTEEN

THE SHEPHERD OF

Blessings

"MY CUP OVERFLOWS"

THE DAY A TOWN BECAME JEWISH

Ed's parents divorced when he was ten, and his ten-year-old friend, Danny, extended his hand to the floundering boy. They lived next door to each other, studied and played together as best friends do, and learned the values of Jewish community. They grew up knowing that every Jewish neighborhood must have a kosher butcher shop, the public school system should close because of lack of attendance on high holy days, and schoolteachers should speak with either European or Israeli accents.

There was an air of superiority in the boys' Jewish world. They were not to "mix" too much

For where two or three come together in my name, there am I with them.
—Matthew 18:20

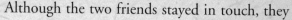

with the non-Jewish community. Dating a non-Jew would cause the kind of anguish associated with divorce—or worse yet—some type of disease.

Although the two friends stayed in touch, they eventually went separate ways. Ed remained involved in Jewish synagogue life, eventually becoming a rabbi. Although Danny's father, Samuel, came from a distinguished line of rabbis, Danny went to college, attended an Ivy League law school, and married Margaret, who was not Jewish. They had two sons, Noah and William. Aside from teach-

ing Noah, the older son, to read Hebrew letters, Danny taught his sons no Hebrew. Their observance of Judaism consisted largely of having a Seder once a year in remembrance of Passover. Danny and Margaret settled in a Kentucky town of three thousand non-Jewish people that had no synagogue or other Jewish institution.

Danny worked with the Legal Services

Corporation providing legal aid until he was diagnosed with cancer. At first he was confident, but none of the various treatments he received had worked. At that point Danny asked Margaret to call Ed.

Ed arrived late that same evening. Upon entering the town, he said aloud to himself, "What in the world is he doing here? Why did he choose to spend his life in this God-forsaken town? There are no Jews here." He became angry about Danny's decisions as he drove to Danny's farmhouse a mile outside of the gone-in-the-blink-of-an-eye downtown in the middle of nowhere. Cancer had spread throughout Danny's body, and he could not move without the support of a walker and his wife. He lay on the sofa, heavily medicated for pain, but smiled when he saw his dear friend.

"How are you doing with all this?" Ed asked.

Danny smiled again and, with great effort,

explained his last request of Ed. "I want a traditional Jewish funeral. Would you help make this possible?"

"Sure, Danny," answered Ed with a moment of hesitation. "I'll help you."

The next day, Margaret invited Steve—a local carpenter—to their home to discuss building a casket. In the dining room, Ed explained to Steve that according to Jewish law a casket should not be made of metal. He explained the Jewish belief that one's life arises from the dust and returns to the dust, so materials that decompose in the earth over time were required. If possible, pine should be used and there should be little ornamentation.

"I've never done this before," Steve responded. "I'll do my best." He rose to go to Danny's room, turned, and asked, "Can I use honey oak instead of pine and carve a six-pointed star on top?"

"Of course," Ed answered.

After talking to Steve he went to the funeral home. "You will need to remove all symbols of Christianity," he told the funeral director. He also explained about the shrouds—the traditional, white burial garments worn by the deceased. The director said if Ed would obtain them, the staff would do their best to prepare Danny's body. He then explained to Ed that they had never had a Jewish funeral before. In fact, people in the community had never been to a Jewish funeral, so Ed might have to take it slow and keep things simple.

Five days after Ed returned home, Danny died surrounded by his family. Steve called Ed about Danny's Hebrew name in order to carve it on the casket. Ed took out a Jewish Bible, made a copy of Danny's Hebrew name, *Dahyniel ben Sh'muel*, cut and pasted the words together, and faxed them to Danny's law office.

Ed arrived late Wednesday, bringing traditional

burial garments: fifty *yarmulkes* (skull caps), a few funeral booklets, and a *shiva* candle. Driving past church after church, he wondered, "Can Danny's last wish be fulfilled?"

Later, at the funeral home, the director and Ed discussed the service. In the room where the service would be held, Danny lay in the casket, the lid in place as Ed had requested. The beautiful casket was stained and had a Jewish star on top. Underneath the star was Danny's Hebrew name, carved perfectly in Hebrew characters.

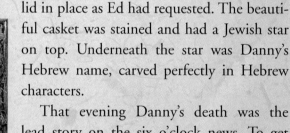

That evening Danny's death was the lead story on the six o'clock news. To get away from the grief-laden atmosphere and review details for the following day, William, Noah, and Ed took a walk. The boys were worried about the service and their obligation to recite the *Kaddish*, the prayer for those who suffer the loss of a family member.

Ed assured the boys that it would be a small service and that they would do well. "Besides," he added, "the only Jews who will be there are your grandmother, me, your aunt and uncle, a nephew and cousins, and your father's supervisor. As it turned out, none of what occurred that day prepared Ed for what happened next."

Two hundred people attended Danny's funeral service. Although only eight Jews attended, all fifty *yarmulkes* were used. Ed explained each step—from the traditional tearing of the garment to symbolize the beginning of the mourning period—to the prayer seeking God's compassion for Danny's soul. Ed did not omit any Hebrew. When the congregation came to Psalm 23, everyone recited, "The Lord is my shepherd," softly. With fifty *yarmulkes* clearly visible, the townspeople mourned the loss of their only Jew.

Ed began to take comfort as he marveled at the turnout. When Danny's boss spoke, Ed learned

The hardest arithmetic to master is that which enables us to count our blessings.
—Eric Hoffer

why so many people had come. Danny had made a huge contribution to that community. From protecting parental rights to civil rights cases involving sexual and racial discrimination, Danny's list of accomplishments in the small, conservative community was formidable. Yet Danny had sel-

dom talked about them when talking with Ed. Clearly he had pursued the principle of *tzedek, tzedek, tirdoph,* "justice, justice, you shall vigorously pursue" mentioned in Deuteronomy 16:20. He had lived his life fulfilling one of the highest Jewish precepts found in the Torah (the Law) and had carried the mantle of his ancestry effectively at its very essence.

When the pallbearers began to move the casket to the hearse, everyone stood as if given a cue. Ed asked those who were going to the burial site—a small stretch of land situated thirty miles from the funeral home—to remain. All two hundred people sat down quietly and waited for what came next.

"Each of you can choose to throw a shovelful of dirt onto the casket at the end of the burial service," Ed said. "Then you will form an aisle for Danny's family to walk through to their cars while reciting the Hebrew phrase, *Hamakom y'nachem m'avlei tziyon*, which means 'May God comfort you among the mourners of Zion.'"

Fifty cars drove in the long procession. At the cemetery, the casket was lowered. During the *Kaddish*—the liturgical prayer— Ed looked over at Noah and William. John had his arms around one boy, Margaret's arms were around the other, and the boys' lips moved to the traditional words. Although Danny was dead, the essence of his wish was being fulfilled; William and Noah were saying the *Kaddish*.

Margaret shoveled the first dirt, followed by her

family. Everyone present fulfilled the commandment of helping Danny to return to the earth from which he had come. Immediately the Christians in this Kentucky town formed an aisle. As Danny's family walked between them, they repeated the traditional words of comfort to those who mourn.

They performed *g'milat hesed*, a righteous act. During that moment, an entire town became a part of *k'lai yisrael*, a Jewish community, granting Danny's desire for a traditional Jewish funeral.

An entire town participating in Jewish rituals didn't take away Ed's grief. It did, however, answer the question he'd asked himself as he initially drove into Danny's town.

When we lose one blessing (Danny was a blessing to Ed and everyone who knew him), another is often unexpectedly given in its place. The Shepherd gave Ed, and the town, a blessing that day in 1994 as they laid their dear friend to rest. The Shepherd gave the town the blessing of being able to honor Danny in a profound way that touched their lives.

The measure of life, after all, is not its duration but its donation.
—Peter Marshall

Then make my joy complete by being like-minded, having the same love, being one in spirit and purpose.
—Philippians 2:2

SHOWERS OF BLESSING

FANNY CROSBY

Here in Thy Name we are gathered,

Come and revive us, O Lord;

"There shall be showers of blessing,"

Thou hast declared in Thy Word.

CHAPTER FOURTEEN

THE
SHEPHERD WHO
Loves

> **"SURELY GOODNESS AND LOVE WILL
> FOLLOW ME ALL THE DAYS OF MY LIFE"**

SCARLET MEMORIES AND YELLOW PANTIES

My father died unexpectedly of an aneurysm. He died alone instead of being surrounded by his eight offspring and twenty-plus grandchildren. There's something shocking about not being able to say good-bye to someone you love. Worse than the sudden loss was feeling that I hadn't let my father know the depth of my love. I'd last seen him at my brother's funeral two years earlier. I had called home every now and then and had meant to visit him, but due to challenging finances, I couldn't afford the trip until it was too late and all too necessary.

I have loved you with an everlasting love; have drawn you with loving-kindness.

—Jeremiah 31:3

With characteristic organizational skill, my sister, Debbie, took charge. She and my other sisters, Diane and Patricia, drove up from Texas with their families. They cleaned out my father's apartment in Topeka, Kansas, and, along with my mother, made necessary arrangements. I did what I could from halfway across the country in Florida.

Before the funeral we all shared stories and memories of our handsome, intelligent father who never quite lived the life he had wanted. We laughed and cried as is customary when families gather to mourn.

Our father had loved music of all sorts. He had sung beautifully and played the saxophone (not quite so beautifully). He had visions of his four daughters being even more famous than the Lennon Sisters. We had watched every variety show from Ed Sullivan to Carol Burnett, with *Ted Mack's Amateur Hour* and *The Miss America Pageant* thrown in for good measure.

As we all reminisced about Daddy, we thought of the many concerts we four daughters had given in the living room. We had sung for every occasion and had a complete repertoire.

I'd volunteered to sing during the funeral, and, much to my surprise I made it through two hymns without crying. I was fine through the Scripture readings and testimonies from family, friends, and church members. I even handled the eulogy without much trouble. Emotions have a way of sneaking up, though, and that's exactly what happened to me.

Right before the service ended, my three sisters sang a song so loved by my father "Scarlet Ribbons." I didn't know it was going to happen and was unprepared for my explosion of emotions followed by a thunderstorm of tears. My tears didn't stop, even when the service did, and then we headed to the cemetery.

I couldn't get that haunting melody out of my

head as I sat at the graveside. I wasn't remembering the version I'd just heard but the one that the four of us had sung so many years earlier while wearing our matching dresses. Then a slide show of remembrances flooded my mind.

First I thought of Daddy's birthday the year I turned four. My mother had told me, "You don't always have to buy a gift for someone you love. You can do a favor, or even give him something special of yours you think he might like." So I took that wisdom to heart. That evening, as the smudged paper came off the crushed box, the lid fell off, revealing yellow fabric. Daddy's resonant laughter boomed through the small living room, while my sisters' shrill giggles nearly drowned out another brother's chuckle. I ran upstairs to hide.

My mother followed me and quietly sat down on my bed. "What's wrong, Carmen?" she asked.

"Daddy didn't like my gift," I replied, sobbing. "He

laughed at me and so did everyone else. Even you. You said I could give Daddy something of mine I liked best of all. I never even wore those panties before. He doesn't like them, and he doesn't like me."

"Honey, those yellow panties with all the ruffles are beautiful, but daddies don't usually wear ruffled panties, and they really are very tiny."

The party was ruined for me. I stayed in my room and cried myself to sleep. The yellow panties were never mentioned again.

Next I remembered a scene when I was nine. I had peeked into the French doors of my parents' bedroom. Through the sheer curtains and small windowpane, I saw my dad wearing a burgundy suit and a hat curved downward toward his handsome features. He stooped defeatedly and carefully placed his clothing in a scarred, leather suitcase.

Our parents had told us that they were getting a divorce and Daddy would be living somewhere else. Divorce was quite rare in the 1960s. As is

I know for certain that we never lose the people we love, even to death. . . . Their love leaves an indelible imprint in our memories.
—Leo Buscaglia

often the case with young children, I decided instantly that the blame was mine. My father was leaving because of something I'd done.

Just as I pulled away from the glass, a flash of yellow caught my eye. He had packed the ruffled panties! I knew then just how much Daddy loved

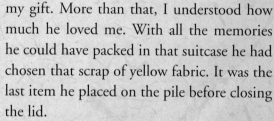

my gift. More than that, I understood how much he loved me. With all the memories he could have packed in that suitcase he had chosen that scrap of yellow fabric. It was the last item he placed on the pile before closing the lid.

After the funeral I flew home, happy I'd seen my family but angry with myself and feeling guilty. *How can I know that my father understood how much I loved him?* I thought. *Why didn't I call and write more and visit him?* I also felt sadness and a constant feeling of aloneness that surprised me.

A few weeks later, on the way to the mall

to buy a baby gift for a friend's daughter, I again found myself thinking about my father. A renewed sense of guilt grew as I remembered how much he had wanted me to come and sign copies of my first book at the Topeka library. *Why did I find a way to make it back for the funeral instead of doing it when he was alive and it would have mattered much more?*

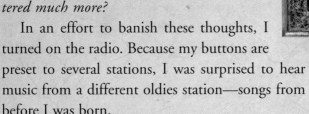

In an effort to banish these thoughts, I turned on the radio. Because my buttons are preset to several stations, I was surprised to hear music from a different oldies station—songs from before I was born.

Still wondering if my absence had made my father doubt my love for him, I pulled into a parking spot. Just as I started to turn off the engine I heard the familiar strains of "Scarlet Ribbons." Before the funeral I hadn't heard that song for decades, but now it was playing on a radio station I never listened to. I sang along until the song ended, then went into the mall.

Still feeling guilty, I took the escalator upstairs, walked into the toddler's section, and began to cry. There, on top of a small pile of clothes, not even where they belonged, was a pair of yellow, ruffled panties. It was as if my father had  dropped those panties from heaven as a way of letting me know that I could quit worrying. He had loved me when I was four, and when I was nine, and he loved me still.

When I needed them most, the Shepherd gave me two affirmations. I didn't buy a present that day, but I did savor my gift; the gift of love. I walked to my car content with the knowledge that not only did my father love me, but so did the Shepherd. He loved me enough to give me memories of "Scarlet Ribbons" and yellow panties.

*Death is the end of a life,
not the end of a relationship.*
—Mitch Albom

I will not leave you as orphans; I will come to you.
—John 14:18

O, HOW I LOVE JESUS

FREDERICK WHITFIELD

It tells of One whose loving heart

Can feel my deepest woe;

Who in each sorrow bears a part

That none can bear below.

CHAPTER FIFTEEN

THE
SHEPHERD OF
Joy

"AND I WILL DWELL IN THE HOUSE OF THE LORD FOREVER"

THE DAY HEAVEN TOUCHED EARTH

When the doctor told Dorothy and Herrick that his problems were probably caused by Alzheimer's disease, they were stunned. They had expected to hear that whatever was causing his memory and logic-related difficulties could be treated with some sort of medication. Instead they learned that he was already in the moderate stage of the illness that would change his personality and rob him of more than they could possibly imagine.

The Alzheimer's diagnosis blindsided them and slammed the door on their retirement plans. Grieving for her husband became a way of life for

Do not grieve, for the joy of the LORD is your strength.
—Nehemiah 8:10

Dorothy. One day, while preparing lunch in the kitchen, she experienced a heartbreaking moment.

"Who am I?" asked the man she had married fifty years earlier. "What's my name?"

"Your name is Herrick," answered Dorothy as calmly as possible. "I am your wife, and we love each other."

"Good. I don't have to worry then," responded Herrick.

As soon as she could, Dorothy went into the bathroom, shut the door, and cried over this loss and those that would follow. She tried not to think about the future and what it would be like, but at times her fears inevitably surfaced.

"Help me to trust you," Dorothy would pray when she felt she couldn't continue. "Help me to find joy in the midst of this terrible disease."

With the Shepherd's help, Dorothy focused on joyful times she and Herrick had shared. Even as she wondered how she could scale the impenetrable walls that were imprisoning her husband's brain, she remembered that he was still the same person. Those memories helped her to say "I love you" at least once a day.

Several years after they had learned the news, Herrick could say very little and almost never put words together to form a sentence. One Sunday morning after getting dressed for church, Dorothy walked in to tell Herrick good-bye. As she entered the room where her daughter and Herrick were sitting, he looked at her and spoke words that Dorothy thought she would never hear again: "You're the most beautiful thing I have ever seen."

In the past, he had often told her she was pretty and looked nice. But sincere words, spoken against all odds, still overwhelmed her. These words comprised one of the best and last gifts he gave Dorothy, and she still treasures them.

After eight years of watching the disease steal her husband bit by bit, there came a day when Herrick quietly and slowly drew his last breath. Dorothy felt as if a part of her had been torn away. This new grief was different; it was final and permanent. Yet as she stood by his bedside, Dorothy knew without a doubt that the Shepherd was nearby. It seemed as if he were saying, "All is well. You don't have to be afraid."

As Dorothy sat beside her deceased husband, she rejoiced that Herrick was now whole and beyond the clutches of Alzheimer's disease. The Shepherd of joy, she felt, had greeted Herrick as he entered heaven.

The joy of knowing where a loved one is for eternity is a gift only the Shepherd can give. Let me share another story of how God gave a life-changing message to someone else who faced a loved one's battle with Alzheimer's disease.

One day, accompanied by her mother and aunt,

twelve-year-old Karen visited her beloved grand-mother, Mary, in the nursing home. Years of being a faithful Christian had ingrained God's Word into Mary's brain. Instead of the empty ramblings that some people suffering from Alzheimer's disease utter, Mary recited Scriptures and hymns. With a joy shaped by years of intimacy with the Shepherd, she'd sing "Just As I Am" despite her muddled mind.

In addition to having Alzheimer's disease, which had left her a gaunt shell of herself, Mary suffered from such severe arthritis that her face seemed to be a mask of pain. Her hands had frozen into two cramped claws, and she could no longer lift her arm more than a couple of inches.

That day, however, Karen witnessed something that brought joy in the midst of her sadness. As she started to turn away from the bed, she was filled with an emotion unlike anything she had felt before. "Look, look," she exclaimed pointing. "Look at Grandma. She has this huge smile on her face."

Before anyone could comment, Mary's hand slowly began to move. Little by little, her fingers on one hand straightened as her arm rose.

Karen, along with her mother and aunt, stood mesmerized as Mary's hand stretched higher and higher. Her chin rose as if looking up. Just as she started to ask why her grandmother was looking toward the ceiling, Karen imagined a hand coming down from heaven. Her grandmother's face glowed as the Shepherd reached down and gently cradled her outstretched hand into His. In a few seconds, Mary was pulled almost to a sitting position. A few seconds later, she fell limp back into the bed.

That moment Karen saw joy replace her grandmother's pain and confusion as Jesus' nail-scarred hand lifted Mary toward heaven. During the decades since then, Karen's faith in the Shepherd has never wavered. She still remembers the joy she experi-

Joy is not the absence of suffering. It is the presence of God.
—Janet Erskine Stewart

enced that day and during the funeral. As Mary lay in her casket she still smiled. The hand touched by the Shepherd remained straight, looking years younger than its gnarled twin. The joy of feeling and seeing the Shepherd's presence and glory offset Karen's grief. When we lose someone we love, the joy of knowing that they are in heaven waiting for us brings us joy. One day heaven will touch earth for us and we will join our loved ones in a joyful celebration.

Never let anything so fill you with sorrow as to make you forget the joy of the Christ risen.
—Mother Teresa

*But let all who take refuge in you be glad;
let them ever sing for joy. . . .*
—Psalm 5:11

HE HIDETH MY SOUL

FANNY CROSBY

He hideth my soul in the cleft of the rock

That shadows a dry, thirsty land;

He hideth my life with the depths of His love,

And covers me there with His hand,

And covers me there with His hand.

"I would say to those who mourn . . . look upon each day that comes as a challenge, as a test of courage. The pain will come in waves, some days worse than others, for no apparent reason. Accept the pain. Do not suppress it. Never attempt to hide grief from yourself."
—Daphne du Maurier

Carmen Leal knows the comfort that only the Shepherd can bring during times of intense grief. She is the author of six books, including *The Twenty-Third Psalm for Caregivers*, *Faces of Huntington's*, and *Portraits of Huntington's*. A storyteller who has a dramatic testimony, she is a popular presenter at women's retreats, church groups, conventions, and conferences.

For more grief-related resources, please visit:
http://www.thetwentythirdpsalm.com

Thank you to those who graciously shared the intimate and painful details of the times when the Shepherd walked you through a valley. Your stories give others hope.

Is death *the last* sleep? No, it is *the last* final *awakening.*

—*Sir Walter Scott*